Lindsy

Revenge

C000192917

Revenge was Howard B   st
of his work to be seen in London — at the Royal Court Theatre
Upstairs in 1969. Adam Hepple, a petty criminal with delusions
of grandeur, finishes a stretch in Brixton gaol and sets about
avenging himself on MacLeish of the Yard, the police commissioner who has dogged his career. When Hepple shoots an
ordinary copper, it is MacLeish's turn for revenge.

　　This tale of twin avengers, written in the larger-than-life comic-
grotesque style that hall-marks Brenton's early plays, is given an
added twist by having both Hepple and MacLeish played by the
same actor.

*The front cover photograph shows a scene from the Royal Court
Theatre Upstair's 1969 production of* Revenge, *and is by Douglas
Jeffery. The photograph of Howard Brenton on the back cover is
by Snoo Wilson.*

Howard Brenton

REVENGE

METHUEN · LONDON

First published in Great Britain 1970 by Methuen & Co Ltd,
11 New Fetter Lane, London EC4P 4EE
Re-issued in this edition 1982 by Methuen London Ltd
Copyright © 1970, 1982 by Howard Brenton

ISBN 0 413 50010 1

ACKNOWLEDGEMENT
The lines by e.e. cummings quoted in Scene Ten are taken from
'in just' which is included in COMPLETE POEMS, published in
the United Kingdom by MacGibbon and Kee Ltd and in the
USA and Canada by Harcourt Brace and World.

Acknowledgement is made to both publishers. It should be noted
that the lines are not reproduced here as written by e.e. cummings
but are deliberately misquoted for dramatic effect.

Set in IBM 10pt Journal by ⌐ Tek-Art, Croydon, Surrey
Printed in Great Britain by Richard Clay (The Chaucer Press) Ltd,
Bungay, Suffolk

Revenge was first performed at the Royal Court Theatre Upstairs on 2 September, 1969 with the following cast:

ADAM HEPPLE	John Normington
VOICE OF BRIXTON GAOL	Barry Lineham
ROT	Bill Stewart
BUNG	Paul Brooke
P C GEORGE	Barry Lineham
P C ALBERT, later the GHOST OF P C ALBERT	Timothy Block
LIZ	Ursula Mohan
JANE	Pamela Moiseiwitsch
ASSISTANT COMMISSIONER ARCHIBALD MACLEISH	John Normington
DAISY, a Cow	Ursula Mohan
	Bill Stewart
COWHAND	Timothy Block
DOROTHY MACLEISH	Ursula Mohan

Directed by Chris Parr
Designed by Philip Jordan
Stage Director Nick Heppel

Act One

Scene One

Before Brixton's Gate.

HEPPLE, *as if thrown on. He's a dirty old man and carries a parcel.*

From the side, the VOICE OF BRIXTON GAOL.

BRIXTON GAOL. Adam Hepple, hear me.

HEPPLE (*mumble*). Bah. Knotted. Get knotted. Knotted right up.

BRIXTON GAOL. Adam, I am the Voice of Brixton Gaol. Once more you are issuing forth into Society from my grey interior.

HEPPLE (*mumble*). Rubbish.

BRIXTON GAOL. You just done eight years, Adam. And it's not the first time you've done, not by a long chalk. Ah, Adam, review your prospects. Half a lifetime in custody and what now?

HEPPLE (*mumble*). Balls, the lot of it. Pontificating balls. Balls, balls.

BRIXTON GAOL. Grief, Adam, that's what it'll be the next time around. Adam, be reconciled to your dreary lot. Burden the taxpayer no more. Commit no further criminal act or it'll be grief, and the nick forever.

HEPPLE (*aloud*). Get your public arsehole knotted, you shithouse. There's life in the old dog yet. I was big once, I'll be big again.

BRIXTON GAOL. Hark not back to the 1940's.

HEPPLE. Ha! That makes you tremble don't it, shake right down to your lime pit, don't it. I will be big again, but big, big, bigger. I have been a life-long admirer of the works of Al Capone. I'll bring the days of Al to England's green and pleasant. Holborn, Waterloo, Notting Hill and Kensington, cars burning in the streets, bullets ripping up the flowerbeds. I'll be a one-man crime wave, once I get going. I just got to get going, that's all.

BRIXTON GAOL. Abandon these senseless dreams.

HEPPLE. Never! I'll bring them all to pass. And the first will be revenge on the dick who shopped me.

BRIXTON GAOL. Not MacLeish of The Yard.

HEPPLE. MacLeish!

BRIXTON GAOL. Oh, Adam, you lost soul, MacLeish is the best loved copper in the land.

HEPPLE. MacLeish! The very name of that Scotch rozzer turns me over. He was the first. You know that? The first ever to say: 'Are you coming quietly?' I was seventeen and thieving in Woolworths, he was a police cadet doing his Ma's shopping. He deflowered my criminal virginity and he's been doing it ever since. It turns me over to recollect the jobs I was about to pull when that scabby jock came on the scene. I'm gonna stuff his truncheon right up his highland fling for good. Ha!

(*To the* GAOL:) Ta ta, you crapsmeared heap of judgement.

HEPPLE *goes off.*

BRIXTON GAOL. Oh, England what will become of you if you turn out foul old men like this.

Scene Two

Billiard Hall.

ROT *and* BUNG *playing snooker.*
ROT *a dated spiv, but fancy.*
BUNG *is massive, thick, often fiercely concentrating. No need for a table, etc. They have cues, and mime the table and the shots.*

ROT *plays a number of smooth shots, with affected movements.*
BUNG *watches the movements of the balls hard.*

ROT (*fails*). Fuck. Your break.

BUNG. What?

ROT. Your turn.

BUNG. Oh, yeh.

BUNG *approaches the table, the cue held the wrong way round.*

ROT. Eh.

ROT *indicates 'turn the cue round'.* BUNG *does so with:*

BUNG. Oh, yeh.

BUNG *winds himself up, a slamming shot.*
Pause.
They look at each other, ROT *with infinite suffering.*
They kneel down to find the balls under the table.
HEPPLE *comes on while they're on their knees.*

HEPPLE. Hello, Rot.

Pause.

ROT. Adam.

Swallow.

I thought you were dead.

HEPPLE. Very much not, Rot.

ROT. Get out today, did you?

HEPPLE (*nothing*).

ROT. Well, this is a nice surprise.

HEPPLE. You not changed much in eight years, Rot. Still totally insincere.

ROT. You look well too, Adam.

HEPPLE. You little cunt.

ROT. Now, now.

HEPPLE. What I want to know is, when I went into the safe, who closed the door?

ROT (*swallow*). Yeh, about that.

HEPPLE. And when I cut my way out, who told MacLeish's flat feet to be standing there.

ROT. Yeh, about that.

HEPPLE. About that.

ROT. Yeh.

Pause.

HEPPLE. What's that you got there?

ROT. That is my associate. Name of Bung.

BUNG. Yeh?

ROT. Shut up.

BUNG. Sorry.

HEPPLE. Bung?

BUNG. Yeh?

ROT. Shut up.

BUNG. Sorry.

ROT. B-U-N-G. As in bath. Called so cos he stops things. Bung.

BUNG. What you want?

ROT. I said shut up.

BUNG. Sorry.

HEPPLE. Thick, is he?

ROT. He has his limitations. He's a wrestler by profession, but he don't get much work cos he can't remember the holds.

HEPPLE. He's not what I had in mind, but he'll do.

ROT. Do?

HEPPLE. I need a knocker.

BUNG. Knock? Knock? Someone say knock?

Fist gesture.

Knock?

ROT. Oh, shut up. Do your exercises.

BUNG. What?

ROT. Your bulge movements.

BUNG. Oh, yeh, me bulge movements.

He begins his exercises.

ROT. What you want a knocker for?

BUNG. Knock?

ROT (*indicates biceps*).

BUNG (*continues his exercises*).

ROT. Getting a mob together again, eh, Adam? Make a comeback?

HEPPLE. That's it, Mr Rot.

ROT. Straight out the nick, straight into the cut and thrust of everyday criminal life eh? Big time again.

HEPPLE. Big time.

ROT. Big time my aunt's wooden fanny.

HEPPLE. What you say?

ROT. I said big time my aunt's wooden fanny. You sad old man, look at you. The one-time metal king of the 1940's. The man who stole a gunboat out of Portsmouth Harbour and flogged it to the Japs for scrap. Come to this. A limping old crackpot out of the nick for the umpteenth time, clutching his parcels of clothes eight years out of date and his Samaritans Bible. Oh, Adam, your time's long gone. All your old buddies, they're all dead. Or sitting in the House of Lords.

HEPPLE. I'll have another gang, mean and deadly, eyes of steely blue, biceps like wires. Men without a moral sense of responsibility. Vicious and smiling. A fancy shirted lot with a love of cats and kiddies, but a murderous knowledge of knives. I'll have 'em again.

ROT. The Adam Hepple Super Gang.

HEPPLE. Right. You an' him are founder members.

Pause.

BUNG *has continued his exercises.*

ROT. For fuck's sake, stop jigging up and down.

BUNG. Sorry.

Stops.

ROT. You're not serious. I am the lowest of the low. I live off other people's fags. I have a nervous complaint that makes me chicken out at the slightest whiff of trouble. I do odd jobs. Very odd jobs if the money's right. I am a parasite on the criminal classes. I have sold my grandma up and down the river so often she thinks she's a fish. All that I am, BUT I am not the bumboy of a gaga old gaolbird.

HEPPLE. That you may not be. But you are a grass.

Pause.

ROT. Now, Adam, let's not lose our heads. Let's discuss this reasonably, one thieving bastard to another.

HEPPLE. You snivelling sneak, you telltale grass.

ROT. Don't call me that word. You give me a nervous flush.

HEPPLE. I'll give you flush. Right down the john. Scatter you
for sewage in the Thames, you shitcake. You tipped off
MacLeish.

ROT. It was an accident. I was nervous. I slammed that safe
door before I knew what I was doing.

HEPPLE. Phoned Whitehall 1212 by accident too? Phone sort of
sprang out the kiosk into your hand by accident?

ROT. You knew I was unreliable. You ought never to have got
me on a job like that. I have a very sensitive skin, prison
clothes would ruin it.

Wipes his brow.

See, the very mention of prison sends me pores mad, pouring
out sweat. I couldn't stand imprisonment. Screws standing
in the lavatory door while you're doing your business. I'd die,
die.

Change.

Right, I grassed on you. I tipped MacLeish his old enemy was
stuck in a safe in the Tottenham Court Road. It was your
fault. I was all you could get, wasn't I! No self-respecting
criminal would work with Mr Big-time Hasbeen.

Change.

Oh, Adam, I'm not denigrating your past achievements. You're
in the annals of villainy, all right. They still use your name to
frighten young bogies with. Be content with that. Retire.
Put your feet up. Fade away with dignity.

Pause.

HEPPLE *walks round* ROT *and* BUNG. *Stops near* BUNG.

HEPPLE (*deliberately*). If HE told YOU to screw MY head off,
what would you do?

BUNG (*thinks, then*). I'd screw your head off.

HEPPLE. Cos he's your friend.

BUNG. He's my friend.

ROT. What you up to, Adam . . .

HEPPLE. Wrestler, are you?

BUNG. What?

HEPPLE. Tear your enemies apart, do you?

BUNG. I tear my enemies apart.

HEPPLE. A real Godzilla.

BUNG. What?

ADAM. A monster out the fabled past. Crushing men between your fingers, crushing buildings between your teeth, a real King Kong, that you?

BUNG. I dunno. I wrestle under the name of the Hairy Ape.

HEPPLE. A man after my own heart. Primeval man, primitive, a real neanderthal.

Pause.

BUNG. What?

ROT. No good, Adam. He's my knocker. Answers to me and to no other.

HEPPLE. Bung. Know who I am?

ROT. He'll pulverise you, Adam. I've only got to give the word and he'll pulverise you.

HEPPLE. Know who I am, Bung?

BUNG. Some old git.

HEPPLE. I am Mick MacManus's Dad.

Pause.

BUNG. Mick's Dad?

HEPPLE. Mick's my boy.

ROT. What a pathetic gambit. You great heap, he's lying.

BUNG. Mick's Dad! He's one of the greats, Mick, in't he? Mick. Cor.

HEPPLE. One of the greats, and I'm his Dad.

BUNG. Pleased to meet you, Mr MacManus.

HEPPLE. Pleased to meet you, Bung.

HEPPLE's *hand out, they shake.*

ROT. You gristle head. He's having you on.

HEPPLE. Tell you what, Bung, how you like to meet Mick in the ring?

BUNG. Meet Mick?

HEPPLE. Be a great match. We'll hire the Albert Hall. What an earthquake of a contest. They'll have to reinforce the roof.

BUNG. Cor.

HEPPLE. What do you say?

BUNG. I dunno. Mick's right out of my class.

HEPPLE. The modesty of the man of iron. The humility of the killer. Lad, you've got it.

BUNG. Have I?

HEPPLE. The minute I came in this low den, I could see you have got it. That eagle eye on the billiard ball, that catlike poise. That control of sinew waiting to POUNCE.

BUNG (*starts*).

HEPPLE. A deal then. Mick v. The Hairy Ape in the Albert Hall.

Hand out.

BUNG. Yeh.

They shake again.

BUNG. Will the telly be there?

HEPPLE. Royalty will be there, my Bungle.

BUNG. Yeh, but will the telly be there?

HEPPLE. It will. In colour.

BUNG. Colour telly! I'll have to work up a tan.

ROT. Bung, Bung.

BUNG. Yeh.

ROT. Bung, Bung.

BUNG. Yeh.

ROT. BUNG.

BUNG. HELLO.

ROT. Are you or are you not my boon companion, my

right-hand man, my shield of meat 'tween me and likely trouble?

BUNG. Er . . .

ROT. I done a lot for you, Bung. Who nicked the frozen chicken from David Greigs to keep you fed? Who tucked you up with many a story of a wrestling bout? Who sponged you down? Who put steak on your eye? Who retrieved your gum guard from under the feet of ringside fans? Who darned your monster socks, who got you a tart when you felt in sentimental mood? Rotty Rot, your friend.

BUNG. My friend.

ROT. Do us a favour, Bung. Do your friend a favour.

BUNG. I'll do you a favour.

ROT. I knew you'd do your friend a favour.

BUNG. I'll do you a favour. Just

Searches for the word.

ask.

ROT. See that old man there.

BUNG (*looks around, then sees* HEPPLE).

ROT. Unscrew that old man's head from that old man's body.

Pause.

Unplug that old rubbish head. Plug it back in the nearest light socket so it burns up. As for that old rubbish body, burn that too. So there's nothing left. Just a bit of dirt on the wind, a bit of soot on your finger.

Flicks his finger.

SCREW HIM.

BUNG. Right. 'Ere.

Pause.

That's Mick's Dad.

Pause.

I can't screw Mick's Dad.

Pause.

'Ere.

Pause.

What you want me to screw Mick's Dad for?

Pause.

What you got 'gainst Mick's Dad?

Pause.

I'll tell you what.

Pause.

If you're no friend of Mick's Dad, you're no friend of mine.

Pause. Then as if someone spoke.

What? Yeh.

HEPPLE. Eh, Bung.

BUNG. What, Mr MacManus?

HEPPLE. Do us a favour.

ROT. Oh, no.

HEPPLE. Rot, you are in a predicament.

Smile.

I'll tell you what I'll do. I'll forgive you for grassing on me. There, I've forgiven you. Not only have I forgiven you, but I am letting you back into my gang.

ROT. Oh, no, no.

HEPPLE. I am glad you are delighted. Not many crooks of my class would forgive you, Rot. Some, who shall be nameless, would have you cut up. Cut up and sent to Scotland Yard bit by bit in parcels. But I'm not going to have you cut up and sent to Scotland Yard bit by bit in parcels. Cost a fortune in stamps, anyway. I'm going to give you one more chance.

ROT. Oh, no, Adam, no no no. I've had my chance. I don't want a second chance, Adam. I mean, I've had one chance and you don't get a second chance in life, do you? I've had my chance and that's it. Can't be greedy.

Change.

I don't want anything to do with you, you power-mad old failure.

HEPPLE (*deadly*). You cough out of turn, one cough, and my
friend here, my very very good friend here.

Nods to BUNG.

Hello, Bung, how are you?

BUNG. I'm very well, Mr MacManus.

HEPPLE. Takes you apart and puts you together again. Don't
let that happen. I guess his notions of anatomy are very
crude. And another thing, don't call me Adam. Call me Chief.
No call me Mr Big. No, call me Chief and Mr Big.

ROT (*aside*). I was having a game of billiards. Quite good form.
When in walked death. My game never got back to scratch.

HEPPLE. First call my place. Then when night falls on London
Town, and the Mums and Dads are tucked up and the cats put
out, and the bobby's on his beat and the moon's a mysterious
pallor over the chimney tops, I'll strike my blow, MacLeish.

ROT. Be out in a rash in half an hour.

Sneezes.

A nervous sneeze. I always sneeze nervously when something's
about to go badly wrong.

HEPPLE. Don't hang about. We got offences to commit.

They go off.

Scene Three

GEORGE *and* ALBERT *Put Us Right About the Criminal
Classes.*

GEORGE *and* ALBERT *come on.*
Both PCs, GEORGE *is 41,* ALBERT's *young.*
Helmets off, and smiles to all.

GEORGE. Evening, all. PC George signing on. This here's young
Albert.

ALBERT. Evening all.

GEORGE. A few words for your edification, ladies and gents,
on the nature of the criminal. Now traditionally your
criminal's a foxy dicy snotty-nosed masturbating little runt,

who'd sell his grandma up the river, let alone his country. He starts early, pinching his Dad's fags and his Mum's money for the dinner, and smashing the toys of his brothers and sisters. Next he goes to Borstal for his education, and comes out a right villain, mean and hard, a foxy dicy snotty-nosed masturbating little runt. That is the traditional picture. But unfortunately, as you may have noted, traditions don't go for much nowadays. The times they are a-changing, to coin a phrase. And your criminals are no exception. They're not like the villains of yore, are they, Albert?

ALBERT. No, they're not like the villains of yore.

GEORGE. No, they're not like the villains of yore. You could do a villain of yore cleanly. You could knock him around, tread on his toes, call him names and punch his navel no matter how big he was. In the old days that's what a criminal would want us to do. He'd expect it of us. But now-a-days?

ALBERT. Now-a-days indeed, George.

GEORGE. Now-a-days it's don't you dare touch me and where's my lawyer. In they come to the station full of the citizen's rights and the police a public service and other left wing slogans. It's your comprehensive schools have done it. They don't go to Borstal any more, they go to comprehensive schools. I tell you what you're going to do with your comprehensive education, you're going to educate your criminal classes so much you won't recognise them anymore. And when that day comes we coppers may as well pack up and bugger off to Rhodesia, or South Africa. At least it's clear there who you have to bash. Eh, Albert?

ALBERT. Yes, it's clear there who you have to bash.

They put their helmets back on.

So ladies and gents, be warned. The days of Jack The Ripper, Donald Hume, Heath, Christie, John Haig, Adam Hepple are going. Now the true psychos, the truly vicious nuts and villains don't have names. They look ordinary. As ordinary as anyone. Ladies and gents: look closely at your neighbour, he may be a robber. A trafficker in drugs, an anarchist or a murderer. Don't be fooled just cos he looks like you. That's all.

Nods.

Scene Four

On The Beat.

GEORGE *and* ALBERT *go round on the beat.*

HEPPLE, ROT *and* BUNG *come on.*
BUNG *stops, sniffing.*

HEPPLE. What's the matter?

ROT. He's sensitive to policemen. He can smell their feet.

BUNG. The law's around.

HEPPLE. Piss off casually in the other direction. I don't want
   a confrontation right now.

BUNG. I can smell their feet.

HEPPLE. Oy, fatty.

   Nods him away.

   (*To* ROT:) George, in't it? Still on the beat.

ROT. Too honest for promotion.

HEPPLE. Know the younger one.

ROT. No.

BUNG. I can smell their feet.

ROT. Come on.

BUNG. Cos of my nose.

ROT. Oh, God.

   Suddenly the police look over at the criminals.

   ROT *and* HEPPLE *turn away to hide their faces,* BUNG
   stares back.

   Pause like that.

   Then the criminals go off fast.

   *The police stroll in the same direction, stand at the back,
   checking up.*

   LIZ *and* JANE *come on.*

JANE. I think I fancy (*thinks*) a gypsy tonight. A lovely, oily
   man. What do you fancy, Liz?

LIZ. I don't have fancies. You know that, Jane.

JANE. Someone's got to buy us dinner. May as well be a gypsy. Black hair, rings in his ears and grease all over. Yum yum.

LIZ. We will be bought dinner by a dirty little man in a mackintos as usual. He'll drive an old Ford Anglia. His glasses will be repaired with Elastoplast. As usual.

JANE. Oh, Liz, you are unromantic.

ALBERT. Hello, hello. Crumpet.

JANE. It's funny, scrounging dinner off a man. We scoff all we can while he sits there all agog with sex. Then we nip out the window in the ladies loo. Liz, don't you ever feel sorry, leaving the poor things . . .

LIZ *notices the coppers.*

LIZ. Jane.

JANE. What?

LIZ. A meal's just come round the corner. Freshen up.

JANE *glances at the coppers.*

JANE. Oh.

The girls freshen up, JANE *hitching her tights.*

ALBERT. Hello, hello, indeed. I fancy the wiggly one. Do you know them, George?

GEORGE. I do. You're in for a treat, Albert. Know who they are? The Hepple sisters.

ALBERT. Not the Hepples?

GEORGE. Adam Hepple's daughters.

ALBERT. Cor.

GEORGE. Just relax and do what I do, lad. A copper's got to have a way with these tarts.

Clears his throat.

Hello, girls.

LIZ. Well, look who's here. It's old George.

They go over to him.

LIZ. Ooh, George, what have you got there. Look what he's go there, Jane. A young policeman. In't he nice.

JANE. Ooh, he is nice.

GEORGE. He's called Albert. Albert, this is Liz and this is Jane.

ALBERT. How do you do.

LIZ. Ooh, he's shy. Do you think he's shy, Jane?

JANE. I don't think he's shy. I think he's lovely.

LIZ. But he's blushing.

JANE. I don't mind if he's blushing, it goes with his uniform. You're not shy of me, are you, Albert?

> JANE *touches* ALBERT.

GEORGE (*a loud cough*). How's life then, Lizzie?

LIZ. Terrible. Not got the price of a dinner, have you, George?

GEORGE. That's a bit difficult.

LIZ. Come on, George. For me and Jane.

GEORGE. All right.

> *Gives money on the quiet.*

LIZ. Thank you, George. Do you a favour for that if you like.

GEORGE. Not tonight, Liz.

LIZ. Got your rheumatism again?

GEORGE. It's young Albert here. I should go by the book tonight, he's new.

LIZ. He's a brand new copper?

GEORGE. Policeman, please, Elizabeth.

LIZ. Sorry. He's a brand new policeman?

GEORGE. He is. And he made his first arrest half an hour ago. Only a drunken Irishman, but an arrest all the same.

LIZ. You hear that, Jane? Albert's just arrested someone for the very first time.

JANE. He can arrest me any time. You going to arrest me, Albert, you going to put your shiny new handcuffs on me? Going to lock me up in your cell?

> ALBERT *is stunned by sexy* JANE, *then grabs her and kisses her passionately. They hold the clinch.*

GEORGE (*coughs, then*). Your Dad got out today, didn't he? Turned up yet, has he?

LIZ. He'd better not turn up.

GEORGE. If he does, and he does go on the go again, you'll give me the word.

LIZ. Oh, George, still hoping for promotion.

GEORGE. I'm 41, Liz, still a PC. Out in all weathers deforming my feet. I'm racked with rheumatism. Riding wet bikes has given me terrible piles. I got to get promotion for the sake of my health. It's all right for young coppers like him. 'O' levels all over and smooth talk. Full of yes sir no sir and having sherry with the Super's wife. But an old 'un like me needs a stroke to get noticed. Give us the word, won't you, Liz?

LIZ. I may.

Suddenly ALBERT throws JANE down, himself on her.

GEORGE *coughs.*

GEORGE. Steady there, Albert.

ALBERT *and* JANE *get up, brush themselves down.* ALBERT *straightens his helmet.*

Right, girls. Move along.

LIZ. All right, bye-bye, George.

JANE. Bye-bye, Albert.

ALBERT. Eh — move along.

JANE. Aren't his buttons bright?

The girls go off.

GEORGE. Have to watch yourself, Albert.

ALBERT. Sorry, George.

GEORGE. It's all right having a bit on the side. But the one thing a copper can't do is get carried away. And you very nearly got carried away didn't you?

ALBERT. I'm very sorry, George.

GEORGE. Put it down to experience.

ALBERT. I will.

GEORGE. And remember your Mrs.

They begin a slow walk round on the beat.

How is she, by the way?

ALBERT. Coming on nicely, thank you, George.

GEORGE. How's her cooking?

ALBERT. That's coming on nicely. Though . . .

GEORGE. What.

ALBERT. Nothing. Mustn't grumble.

GEORGE. I dunno. A copper's got to be cooked for properly.

ALBERT. It's her mash. Comes out a bit lumpy.

GEORGE. It's not got lumps?

ALBERT. Sort of grey lumps.

GEORGE. Don't like the sound of that. Can't have you eating lumpy mash, lad. Give you indigestion, seriously hinder your running after criminals. Maybe she's not getting the right potatoes.

ALBERT. King Edwards.

GEORGE. King Edwards should be all right. What's she use for creaming the mash?

ALBERT. Margarine.

GEORGE. Margarine! Well, there you are. My landlady uses double Devonshire cream to which she adds a knob of butter . . .

They're off.

Scene Five

Hepple's Backyard.

The criminals come on.

As BUNG *gets digging with a spade,* ROT *fills the audience in on the situation.*

ROT. Came to his house. Round the back. Into his garden. Nettles everywhere. Old tin cans. Smell of dogshit. Got Bung digging with a rusty spade. I don't like it. I think events are about to take a lurid turn.

HEPPLE. Dig, you fat jelly, dig, you meatball.

BUNG. Right you are.

ROT. What you got down there, Adam? You not got a corpse down there? God, what if he's got a corpse down there? I did not know you went in for that, Adam. I'm surprised at you. I did not think that was your number at all.

BUNG strikes something.

BUNG. 'Ere.

HEPPLE. Strike metal?

BUNG. Something metal.

HEPPLE. My beauty, my beauty!

ROT. He has got a corpse down there.

HEPPLE. Get her up.

ROT. It's a woman. He did a woman in. He's just another Christie. His Al Capone fantasies are just a front.

HEPPLE and BUNG lift up a guncase.

Breathing hard HEPPLE opens the guncase, takes out a machine gun in a cloth, lays back the cloth lovingly.

HEPPLE. My lovely, my deadly lady.

Kisses the gun.

Your prince has come, my love.

ROT. A machine gun not a corpse. That's a relief.

Realises.

A fucking machine gun!

LIZ comes on.

LIZ. Who's out there?

HEPPLE. Hello, Elizabeth.

LIZ. You.

HEPPLE. Lads, meet my eldest. Rot, Bung, Elizabeth, Elizabeth, Rot, Bung.

BUNG. Hello.

ROT. Bonjour, I'm sure.

HEPPLE. Going to give your old Dad a kiss?

LIZ. Why aren't you dead? Why ha'nt they put you in the limepit? Why ha'nt they chopped you up and hung your head in the black museum?

HEPPLE. It's good to be loved by your children. Daughters! I curse the day you started to grow.

LIZ. What's that thing?

Pause.

What's that hideous black thing?

BUNG (*unexpectedly*). That's Mr MacManus's Mash Sheen.

JANE *comes on.*

JANE. Liz, what you doing out there?

And stops.

HEPPLE. Come on, lads. I got what I came for. There's nothing else here for me.

HEPPLE *and* ROT *and* BUNG *go off through the audience.*

JANE. It was Dad. He came home. Do you think he's cured, Liz? They said that on the telly, prison weren't prison now. It's hospital. I look on it like that — Dad was ill, so he went to hospital.

LIZ. A hospital called Brixton Gaol?

JANE. His treatment took ever so long. Eight years long. But they let him out, so he must be alright now. We should have him home, Liz, nurse him while he's convalescent.

LIZ. Oh, Janey, you don't know the half of it. Not the half. Go back inside.

JANE. Going out?

LIZ. You go back inside.

JANE. Where you going?

LIZ. Find George.

JANE. You're not going to shop Dad. Not on his first day.

LIZ. Go and keep warm.

LIZ *goes off fast.*

JANE. He's my Dad. I don't care if he's bad. I'll look after him. Buy him fags, comb his old grey hair, get him crime books from the library. And each night put his teeth in Sterodent and tuck him up, safe as a bug. He's my Dad. Liz, wait . . .

JANE *goes off after* LIZ.

Scene Six

Outside MacLeish's House (i).

Wind noise. ROT *and* HEPPLE *and* BUNG *come on.*

ROT *fills us in about the situation.*

ROT. Garden suburb. Gives me the creeps. Listen. No traffic, no kids. Just the wind in the trees. A very unhealthy sound. All this green in the city, it's not natural.

HEPPLE. That's the house. We'll nip over the fence, get down behind those shrubs and have a look.

(*To* BUNG:) You. Give us a leg.

BUNG *does so.*

ROT. Made straight for this house. Why? I don't like it. My rash is up to my armpits already and my nose is tickling like it was full of feathers. I'm a writhing mass of symptoms of trouble.

HEPPLE. Now him.

ROT. All right, all right I can manage.

BUNG *picks up* ROT, *manhandles him over the fence.*

HEPPLE. And you.

BUNG. Oh, yeh.

Bashes his way through the fence.

They crouch down, looking off at the house.

ROT. It's a big house. Be stuffed to the roof with classy devices against the burglar. You just breathe on a classy house these days and bells go off. And trip wires and yellow dye and dogs trained in karate.

They start.

Lights gone on. That does it. Can't do a house if the occupant's there, can we. Can we?

HEPPLE *says nothing.*

Look, chief, let's go back to what we know. Go down to
Lambeth, eh? Do a chippy, eh? Do a chippy just as they're
closing, eh? That's my plan for the celebration of your release.
I'm not getting chewed up by some karate doing dog, no
thank you.

HEPPLE. We're going to do that house. Not a chippy. That
house. That occupant.

ROT. Oh, God. An horrible intuition is prickling up all over me.
That's MacLeish's house, in't it? That's the house of Assistant
Commissioner MacLeish.

BUNG. Light's gone out.

ROT. Old man, you're dead, you don't live in the world.

BUNG (*sniffs*). 'Ere.

ROT. He's got a scent of approaching coppers. It's all going to
go horribly wrong!

HEPPLE. Get down.

ROT *and* BUNG *and* HEPPLE *crouch down.* GEORGE *and*
ALBERT *come on.*

GEORGE. That's where he lives, God bless him.

ALBERT. It's a lovely house.

GEORGE. That's the reward of fighting the good fight against
wickedness. You fight the good fight against wickedness and
you'll end up with a house like that.

ROT *sneezes. The policemen look at each other.*

GEORGE *nods to* ALBERT *to step back.*

They step back.

GEORGE. I think there's something going on in the Assistant
Commissioner's shrubbery.

ALBERT. Could be lovers.

GEORGE. Could be lovers. Though it's a disgusting thought,
lovers in the Assistant Commissioner's shrubbery.

ALBERT. It is disgusting.

GEORGE. It's disgusting, alright. Let's have a peep.

> GEORGE *and* ALBERT *step forward in unison. They look over the heap of* HEPPLE, ROT *and* BUNG.
>
> *Pause.*
>
> GEORGE *nods to* ALBERT *to step back.*
>
> *They step back.*

GEORGE. I don't think it's lovers. I've got a feeling it's dirtier work than that. I've got a feeling it's dirty work itself.

ALBERT. How do you get that feeling?

GEORGE. Nose, lad. Smell. We've got that in common with them. We can smell their dirty work, they can smell our feet. Have a sniff.

> GEORGE *and* ALBERT *step forward and sniff.*
>
> BUNG *raises his head and sniffs. Then* ROT *and* HEPPLE *sniff.*
>
> *Pause.*
>
> *Police and criminals sniffing.*
>
> *Then* GEORGE *nods to* ALBERT *and they step back.*

Get it?

ALBERT. Sort of sweat.

GEORGE. You got it. Sweat. Your criminal sweats out of fear for his evil deeds. Your peace-loving citizen has no need to sweat. If you're questioning a man and he starts to sweat, book him. They didn't tell you that in Police College, did they? Didn't tell you about the armpits of the underworld, did they?

ALBERT. The training was more theoretical.

GEORGE. Theoretical, my arse.

> *Pause.*

ALBERT. George, I know you've got them on your mind, but what about that lot over there?

GEORGE. I've got them on my mind.

ALBERT. I knew you must have.

> *Pause.*

Shouldn't we do something about them?

GEORGE. We will, lad. We will. We are about to. Yeh, we will.

Pause.

How many do you reckon there are?

ALBERT. How many do you?

GEORGE. Ten.

ALBERT. Ten?

GEORGE. Or fifteen.

ALBERT. That's a lot of felons, George.

GEORGE. That is a lot of felons, Albert.

ALBERT. Shall we tackle them?

GEORGE. Leap over the fence, eh?

ALBERT. Lay them out ourselves.

GEORGE. Us two lay them out. All twenty of them. Better send for reinforcements.

In a hurry GEORGE *and* ALBERT *get their whistles out, blow them.*

ROT *rises in panic.*

The policemen stop blowing and look at him, whistles still in their mouths.

ROT. Nicked! Nicked! God, I'm nicked. Don't let them take me away, Mummy, tell them I'm not bad really, Mummy. I didn't know what I was doing, your honour. I plead unfit to plead, your majesty, oh God. Nicked! Nicked!

HEPPLE. My Rot, what do you think you're doing?

HEPPLE *rises.* GEORGE *and* ALBERT *take their whistles out at the shock of seeing* ADAM.

HEPPLE. Well, if it isn't Police Constable George. Hello, George.

GEORGE. Hello, Adam. You're on the go again, then.

HEPPLE. Keeping well, are you?

GEORGE. Very well, thank you. And you?

HEPPLE. Oh, I'm very happy.

He raises the gun.

GEORGE. Now, Adam, don't do anything rash.

Pause, all eyeing each other.

GEORGE. Albert. RUN, LAD. RUN, LAD.

GEORGE *turns and runs.*

ALBERT *stands there agog.*

HEPPLE. Put your whistle back in your gob, copper . . .

ALBERT *does so.*

HEPPLE *machine guns him.*

ALBERT *sinks slowly to the ground, blowing his whistle.*

The whistle dies away.

He's dead.

Pause.

ROT. What did you do that for? What did you do that for? It's
not happened. Get up, you stupid copper. What you lying in
a pool of blood there for? All right, copper, you can get up
now, you're not really hurt, you're not really riddled full of
holes before our very eyes. We done a copper in. You know
what they do when you do a copper in, they go mad.

At once, many police whistles and sirens off.

BUNG. Eh, eh, thousands of them.

ROT *listens to the whistles then runs off.*

BUNG *stays looking around.*

HEPPLE. My name's on England now. See my name, MacLeish?

Drawing the letters with his toe.

Here in your copper's blood. H-E-P-P-L-E. See my name,
MacLeish, on England and on you?

HEPPLE *raises the machine gun high in a salute.*

BUNG *goes to him, tugs his arm.*

As they turn to run off, lights down fast.

End of Act One

Act Two

Scene One

Outside MacLeish's House (ii)

Whistles and sirens, flashing lights.

ALBERT *lying dead.*

GEORGE *hysterical.*

GEORGE. Mr General Public, have a gawp. Gawp, ooh and aah.
There's a copper dead, here's a copper who ran away. Ooh and
aah, you hypocrites, here we are, one young corpse, one
forty-year-old coward in purgatory with his piles. You got
the police force you deserve, Mr General Public. You turn
me over, you do, turn me over.

Suddenly the whistles die away.

MACLEISH *comes on.*

MACLEISH *is played by the same actor as* HEPPLE.

*He's a Scot, he walks with a stick. He's given to poses. He
wears his overcoat like a cloak.*

MACLEISH. You got a dead copper there.

GEORGE. Assistant Commissioner MacLeish, Sir.

He salutes.

MACLEISH. Let me see the lad.

GEORGE. I'll cordon back the general public. Keep their dirty
eyes off.

MACLEISH. No. Maybe the sight will move their stony hearts.

MACLEISH *kneels by* ALBERT.

GEORGE (*aside*). It was a moving sight. The most moving of all
my years in the Force. The Assistant Commissioner himself
kneeling in prayer beside young Albert's body. There in the
garish lights and the cold night air. I'm not poetical, poetry's
not my bent. But it was beautiful. The great man there
amongst us at the hour of our need and sorrow.

MACLEISH. You noted the letters by his head. The letters there
in the copper's blood. H-E-P-P-L-E?

GEORGE. I blame myself, Sir. I am willing to resign.

MACLEISH. There'll be no resignations. God is working his purpose out. If there were more Christians in the Force you'd know that.

Stands.

I want every road, lane, alley, nook and cranny out the Metropolitan Area blocked.

GEORGE. They are blocked, Sir.

MACLEISH. Airports, docks alerted.

GEORGE. They are alerted, Sir.

MACLEISH. A fresh clean Christian copper gunned down. A young clean upright conservative unarmed Christian copper gunned down. I want every copper in England awake.

GEORGE. They are awake, Sir.

MACLEISH. Albert was his name, wasn't it?

GEORGE. Young Albert, we called him.

MACLEISH. Young Albert. He's with the angels now, clutched to the bosom of Sir Robert himself. I want all the villains told touch Adam Hepple and they're dead. Spread the word.

GEORGE. It's spreading, Sir.

MACLEISH. Then spread it faster.

GEORGE. It's spreading faster, Sir.

MACLEISH. Good man. We'll get the bastard for this. The sight could make a man weep.

Hand out for handkerchief.

GEORGE (*hands him a handkerchief. Aside*): I handed the great man my handkerchief. I never blew my nose on it again. I had the handkerchief framed and it hangs to this day over the mantelpiece in the front room. You can still see the stain the Assistant Commissioner left. And I point it out to visitors and say — that's where MacLeish blew his nose at the scene of the crime.

MACLEISH *blows his nose loudly, hands the handkerchief back.* GEORGE *takes it, looks at it wonderingly.*

MACLEISH. Right, lads. Stir all the muck in England, all the godless villains, stir them. And get the reprobate Hepple.

He sweeps off.

Scene Two

A Street.

LIZ *on.*
JANE *comes on from elsewhere, sees* LIZ.

JANE. Liz. What's up with all the policemen? They've gone potty. Down by Waterloo pie-stall, all these policemen have got all these tramps up against the wall. And you know what, they're all crying.

LIZ. The tramps?

JANE. The policemen, silly. Tears streaming down. They look funny.

LIZ. It's Dad. He's done something. I know! Come home, Jane.

JANE. I want to watch the policemen running around. They look lovely blowing their whistles, their faces go red.

LIZ. Come on, Jane.

JANE. I want to see Albert. I want to blow on his whistle.

GEORGE *comes on.*

He glares at them.

Pause.

LIZ. What's he done, George?

GEORGE. You bitches.

LIZ *makes a move to him.*

Don't come near me, filth. You tarts, get off the street 'fore I run you in.

LIZ. What's he done?

GEORGE. Albert he's done.

JANE. Albert.

GEORGE. Albert he's done. We go mad when a copper's done. Mad with zeal. Knights in shining armour we are when a copper's done, slashing out to right and left, arresting all in sight. So get out my way, trash.

JANE. Our Dad did young Albert?

GEORGE. That's it, girly. Your shitbag father.

JANE. Don't call him that! He did young Albert? Good, good,
I'm glad. He did a copper? Good. He opened up my lovely
Albert's head? Goody good, good for Dad, good for him. Before
you get him, copper, I hope he gets many more of you. Many
many more coppers dead. I hope he covers England with dead
coppers. I hope he leaves us knee deep in coppers, piles of men
in blue blocking up the traffic all dead dead dead.

GEORGE. Chip off the old block, eh? Out of my sight!

LIZ. My poor Janey.

GEORGE. Out of my sight!

Blows his whistle.

LIZ. Come on, there's nothing for our kind here.

She spits at GEORGE.

I share my sister's sentiments. See you in Court, Mr Fuzz.

The girls go off.

GEORGE. Elizabeth . . .

Quietly.

What a lonely job. What a horrible fucking lonely job.

ROT *comes on fast, comes to a full stop on seeing* GEORGE
GEORGE *pulls himself upright.* ROT *decides to brazen it
out. Goes forward.*

GEORGE *goes forward too, and as* ROT *goes past stops him
by linking arms.*

In a hurry, Sir?

ROT. Yes, officer, in a hurry.

GEORGE. A hurry to where, Sir?

ROT. Wife and kids, flatfoot, I mean officer.

GEORGE. What did you call me?

ROT. Officer, officer.

GEORGE. Address.

ROT. One hundred and twenty-eight South Malden Street.

GEORGE. A classy area.

ROT. You could call it classy.

GEORGE. Too classy for you, Rot.

Both stare. Then ROT *makes a break for it.*

GEORGE *chases him off, whistle blowing.*

LIZ *and* JANE *come on, despondent.*

JANE. Liz, I been thinking about Dad. What if he's in a park, or under a bridge. Oh, Liz, we could hide him. That's it. We'll find him and take him home and hide him.

LIZ. And where oh where would we do that?

JANE. In the cellar. I'll clean it out. Make it nice down there. A bit of lino and a rug. A little bed and a comfy chair. No one will ever know. Liz, say yes.

LIZ. You silly little cow. He hates the sight of you. He wants you dead.

JANE. Don't talk like that.

LIZ. He wishes you were never born.

JANE. You're not to talk like that.

LIZ. We're freaks. An accident to him.

JANE. No.

LIZ. When he looks at us, what does he see? Two bad bits of sex he had years ago. Two messes he made.

JANE. You're lying. You're a lying bitch.

LIZ. Come home, Jane.

JANE. No. I'll not live with you anymore. I'll go and find Dad. I've got his skin, you see. His nails. The colour of his eyes is the colour of my eyes. That's family, that's fate. Genetical. I read about that in a magazine, you can't escape your genetical inheritance. Whatever hole he's in I'll live with him there. 'Bye 'bye, Liz.

She goes off.

LIZ. Janey . . .

Aside.

Oh, Dad, you oughtn't to have conceived daughters. I hope you're suffering a bit for conceiving daughters. My poor dirty ratbag father, wherever you are.

She goes off.

Scene Three

Police Station

MACLEISH *asleep in a chair.*

GEORGE *comes on, mimes gingerly knocking at the door, then goes in.*

GEORGE (*salutes*). Sir.

> *No reply from* MACLEISH. *He tiptoes forward and prods him.*

Assistant Commissioner, Sir.

MACLEISH *snorts.*

GEORGE (*springs to attention*). Sir.

> MACLEISH *is still asleep.*

GEORGE (*cautiously prods him again*). Assistant Commissioner, Sir.

MACLEISH (*wakes with a start*). What?

GEORGE (*springs back to a salute*).

MACLEISH. Got him yet?

GEORGE. No, Sir.

MACLEISH. Ah.

> *Pause.*

GEORGE. The Inspector says, Sir, would you care to question the suspect, Sir. The man Rot, Sir.

MACLEISH. What's the time?

GEORGE. 0.400 hours.

MACLEISH. Four o'clock.

GEORGE (*caught out, mental arithmetic*). Four o'clock, Sir.

MACLEISH. We'll let him stew till dawn. A very nasty time for the guilty, the dawn. Very cold.

> *Pause.*

GEORGE (*shuffles*).

MACLEISH. You look worried, constable. What's the matter? Come on, man, we're both coppers, both of the same trade. What's up?

GEORGE. Well, Sir, with respect, Sir, nothing's happening. Sir.

MACLEISH (*looks blank*).

GEORGE. I mean he's getting further away, in't he, Sir?

He swallows.

Hepple. He must be well through the net now and running.

MACLEISH. That's what I want him to do, constable. Run. Run right on till he's in the country. You see, Adam Hepple's heart . . . it's dicky. Didn't know that, did you? I did, I know all about Adam. His heart's strained by years of excess. If he runs hard enough he'll drop down dead of his own accord.

GEORGE. Very clever, Sir.

MACLEISH. It's diabolical, brutal and cruel, and not standard police procedure. But with Adam Hepple you have to be diabolical, brutal and cruel.

GEORGE (*embarrassed, coughs, steps back*). I'll get back to my duties, Sir.

MACLEISH. No. Stay and chat, lad. If you can bear the chat of an old fool.

GEORGE. I'd be pleased to, Sir.

MACLEISH. Pleased to chat with an old fool who happens to be Assistant Commissioner, eh?

GEORGE. No, Sir, yes, Sir.

MACLEISH. Bah.

Pause.

GEORGE. If you'd like a shave, Sir, we have the tackle.

MACLEISH. No, I'll not shave. Al Capone never did. Know that? Al Capone never shaved when he was after a man. When one of his boys was gunned down Al went unshaved until he had revenge. Driving down town the populace would note his grizzled beard, and know well what the stubble on that foul chin meant. Then one morning there'd be a body on the subway or on the shore of Michigan, and Al would be smiling, clean again.

Hoisting himself up.

No, I'll no shave again till Adam's in the pen. Or dead of heart attack.

GEORGE. With respect, Sir, this is England and not Chicago.

MACLEISH. Both foreign parts to a Scot.

Looks sharply at GEORGE, *then:*

You're not by any chance a Calvinist?

GEORGE. Baptist, actually.

MACLEISH. Then you don't know of the Elect.

GEORGE (*gushing*). Perhaps you would care to enlighten me, Sir.

MACLEISH (*looks at him, then*). God, in his wisdom, will on the day of judgement, take to heaven a number of men, that number being 144,000. These men being the Elect, and so from birth, by Divine Ordinance.

GEORGE. But what about the rest of us?

MACLEISH. Damned, Constable.

GEORGE. That's hardly fair, Sir.

MACLEISH. Fair?

GEORGE. How do we know if we're one of the lucky ones, Sir?

MACLEISH. That's the rub. They may all have lived. It could be that our age is every man jack for the fiery pit.

Oddly.

Though I disagree. You see, constable, I know I am one of the number.

GEORGE (*embarrassed*). I see, Sir.

MACLEISH. I am one of the Elect. There's nothing I can do about it, I'm going to see Heaven. You think I'm joking, don't you?

GEORGE. No, Sir. I was just wondering about me.

MACLEISH. You?

Pause.

GEORGE (*coughs*). A very interesting conversation, Sir.

MACLEISH. Your real thought on the conversation is what a load of old cock the old man talks. That your real thought?

GEORGE. I do have difficulty catching the drift of your remarks, Sir.

MACLEISH. What's your name?

GEORGE. PC 149.

MACLEISH. Name not number.

GEORGE. George, Sir.

MACLEISH. Call you Georgy, do they?

GEORGE. No, Sir.

MACLEISH. Do you box, Georgy?

GEORGE. I have donned the gloves, Sir.

MACLEISH. I was Metropolitan Area Middleweight Champion. Know that?

GEORGE. Oh, yes. 1929 by a knockout in the second round.

MACLEISH. Ha! You do know that.

MACLEISH *signals* GEORGE *to come nearer, winds up a punch and punches* GEORGE *in the stomach.*

GEORGE *doubles up a little.*

Ha! Your turn.

MACLEISH *struggles to his feet, stomach out.*

GEORGE. Turn, Sir?

MACLEISH. Turn to strike a blow.

GEORGE. I don't like to, Sir.

MACLEISH. Strike the old man who talks such cock. I'll show you how to win a theological argument. Strike your blow.

GEORGE. I don't like to, Sir. It may not be good for you.

MACLEISH. Constable.

GEORGE. Sir.

MACLEISH. Hit me.

GEORGE *hits him at once.* MACLEISH *doubles up slowly, heavy breathing, almost sinks to the floor, just makes it back to the chair.*

GEORGE. Assistant Commissioner, Assistant Commissioner. Oh, Lord.

MACLEISH. Georgy . . .

GEORGE. Yes, Sir, here I am, Sir, I'm sorry I hit you, Sir . . .

MACLEISH. Pills, Georgy. Inside pocket.

GEORGE. Pills.

MACLEISH. Inside pocket.

GEORGE. Yes, Sir, the pills in your inside pocket, Sir. Oh, where are the bleeders.

Gets them out.

Here they are, Sir.

MACLEISH *gestures for a pill twice.*
GEORGE *gives them to him.*

MACLEISH. It's my heart. As dicky as Hepple's. But his'll go first, won't it, Georgy? His dicky heart will be the first to conk out. Divine justice will see to it. I'm confident his will go first.

GEORGE. His will go first, Sir.

MACLEISH *breathes heavily, then hoists himself up, recovered.*

MACLEISH. What are you looking at, copper? Is it dawn? Thank you for waking me.

GEORGE. Not at all, Sir.

MACLEISH. At the scene of the crime you ran away.

GEORGE. What?

MACLEISH. So not a word of this.

Indicates his heart.

Forget the confidences of a superior officer.

GEORGE *salutes.*

MACLEISH. Get Rot up.

GEORGE. Sir. Get him up.

Voices off: 'get him up, get him up, coming up, coming up, coming up'.

ROT *on at once, as if thrown on.*

ROT. Don't beat me up. I don't know anything about it.

GEORGE *knees him.*

ROT *goes down.*

ROT. Don't beat me up. It was not me. I will make a full
statement. Don't beat me up. It was Hepple and Bung, not me.
I'll tell you all you want and more. I'll lay it on as thick as
you want but don't beat me up. I can't bear violence, I will
make a full and accurate statement, look up the statements
I've made other times. I have helped you with enquiries.
All accurate. I pride myself on my language. Don't beat me
up . . .

GEORGE *puts the boot in.* ROT *continues with 'don't beat
me up' as* GEORGE *does so.*

MACLEISH (*aside*). In Christian times they burnt them. The
Reprobate aflame illuminated the Life of the Chosen. A
truly godfearing experience, to be a copper in the Middle
Ages. No namby pambying. Lop the thieving hand, pluck
the offending eye. Burn! Burn! There were avenging angels
then. Law was divine.

ROT. . . . don't beat me up.

MACLEISH. Does he see the Light?

GEORGE. I'm sorry, Sir?

MACLEISH. Does Rot repent?

GEORGE. The Assistant Commissioner wants to know whether
you repent.

ROT. Yeh yeh, where do I sign?

MACLEISH. Then let us pray. Lord, look down this night on Y
Division. Also look down, oh Lord, on the entire Metropolitan
Area, and beyond that the County Constabularies. Cast thy
all-seeing eye about the streets, the backyards, the highways
and byways. And, oh Lord of Hosts, whatever ditch, chalk
or gravel pit Adam Hepple crouches in, there guide us. That
we may SMITE the slayer of thy servant Albert, Amen.

GEORGE. Amen.

Kicks ROT.

ROT. Amen.

Scene Four

In The Country.

Lights are down.

Birds twittering.

Lights up, a tent, perhaps protruding from a flat, giving an entrance into it that's concealed, as the HEPPLE/MACLEISH *actor has his first quick change here.*

A dead fire, haversacks, tins and mess around.

The tent bulges from inside.

HEPPLE (*inside*). You peabrained elephant, get off my chest.

BUNG (*inside*). Sorry, can't find my socks.

> BUNG *gets out of the tent, stretches, happy, exercises for a bit, goes to one of the haversacks, pours out tins of baked beans and a paperback book.*

My loot. Hello, loot.

Picks up the paperback, reads.

The sel (*pause*) ected poems of e.e. cummings. Yeh, the sel (*pause*) ected poems of e.e. cummings.

Reads sometimes with difficulty and puzzled, but lovingly.

in just spring when the world is mudluscious and the little lame balloon man whistles far and whee. Yeh, whistles far and whee. And eddieandbill come running from marbles and its spring when the world is puddle-wonderful. The queer old balloon man whistles far and whee and bettyandisabel come dancing from hopscotch and jumprope and its spring and the goatfooted balloon man whistles far and whee.

HEPPLE (*head out of the tent*). What are you doing?

BUNG. Reading the sel (*pause*) ected poems of e.e. cummings.

HEPPLE. I thought you couldn't read.

BUNG. No, I can't. But I sort of begun.

Head in hands.

I sort of begun. Dad, You know when we went over that railway running from the dogs. And I tripped up and conked my head? I think it made me read.

HEPPLE (*getting out of the tent*). Conked education into you,
   has it?

BUNG. Indubitably.

HEPPLE (*startled*). What?

BUNG (*startled*). What?

HEPPLE. You came back late last night.

   HEPPLE *is very miserable while* BUNG *goes on — he tries to
   light the fire but the matches are damp, he has a piss upstage
   in a desultory way.*

BUNG. I was out foraging.

   Puzzled.

   Foraging. Yeh, I went out stealing down in the village. Nice
   little houses. Cosy. I never been in the country, it's nice. It's
   like a village on a box of chocs down there. I think I'll be
   a farmer, that would be nice, milking cows, growing tatoes,
   following sheep about with my crook. I'd marry a milkmaid
   and get a good tan. You could be my shepherd. You'd like
   that. You'd have a little shepherd's cottage and a wife who'd
   look after your little lambs when they were born. And we'd
   all be country people.

HEPPLE. You got a bump on that head?

BUNG. Yeh, there is a protrusion.

HEPPLE. Protrusion? Country life? Something's happened to
   you alright. Mister, we're not in the stinking country for
   love of nature. I hate the country. Listen to the bleeding
   birds twittering. Shut up, can't you?

   They don't.

   Little bleeders, twittering on and on. And bleeding cows
   and bleeding sheep and bleeding bulls after sticking their
   horns in your arse. It's not my natural habitat and it's not
   yours, mate. We belong to the streets and pubs and back
   doors, and Leicester Square and the Elephant and Castle.

BUNG. I like the country.

HEPPLE. Be good to be back down at the Elephant. Have a
   pie at Johnny's stall. Do a few tills in the shopping centre.
   Johnny's pies, all hot. I'll have another there, Johnny boy . . .
   Steak sandwich mustard ketchup onions, the lot. Ten days

we been in the country eating grass and snails, and scraps chucked out of cars. We got to eat food.

BUNG. I got some beans. But I forgot to nick a tin opener.

DAISY, *a cow, wanders on.*

Oh, look, a daisy bell.

HEPPLE. Oh, look, a bleeding cow.

BUNG. Hello, Daisy. How your udders, then?

DAISY *backs away a little.*

Don't be afraid of farmer Bung. Farmer Bung won't hurt you.

COWHAND *comes on.* ALBERT *actor doubles this.*

COWHAND. 'Ere. What you doing with that cow?

HEPPLE *picks up the machine gun.*

COWHAND (*backs away*). Who be you?

HEPPLE. We be property developers.

COWHAND. Ah, city folk. How long you been living in my Daddy's field?

HEPPLE. A long time, mister. A very long time.

COWHAND. I not been up here for sometime, you see. Be fallow up here. I'm only up here cos Daisy strayed.

BUNG. Her name Daisy?

COWHAND. It is. Strayed out the milking shed, she did, the naughty titty.

BUNG. 'Ere, can you milk?

COWHAND. Bah, machinery does that now.

BUNG. Machinery?

COWHAND. Lordy, we don't sit on stools and do it with our hands. You have got queer ideas. That's modern farming. Cows is machines. A machine for milk and meat, in't you, Daisy?

BUNG. Don't you love her, then?

COWHAND (*embarrassed*). None of that talk now.

HEPPLE. You. That edible?

COWHAND. ?

HEPPLE. You can eat cows.

COWHAND. Got to slaughter them first. Could bring you a
bit of bread if you're peckish.

HEPPLE. Meat, meat, what about meat?

COWHAND. That's a bit tricky. We not got a Sainsburys in
the village.

HEPPLE. But you're surrounded by meat.

COWHAND. Ain't processed, is it? Maybe I could get you a tin
of spam.

HEPPLE. And a tin opener.

COWHAND. We got all mod cons on our farm. I won't be long.
Don't you go away now.

He goes off, with DAISY.

HEPPLE. All my efforts come to nothing. All my efforts to
brighten up criminal life, sweet nothing. All I wanted to do
was entertain the general public, and make a bit on the side,
naturally. And look at their gratitude — forced out into the
country like a leper. You bleeders, don't you want your
streets full of spectacle and danger?

BUNG (*clutches head, suddenly*). 'Ere. There's a way of life
that's better. Where innocence and guilt they don't apply. It's
just come into my head.

At once, whistles and the police come on.

GEORGE *with a line of cut-out policemen.*

HEPPLE. Where's MacLeish?

GEORGE (*wandering over to pick up machine gun*). Don't start,
Adam. We're all very tired. Been watching you for days.

HEPPLE. Days?

GEORGE. His idea. Hoping that the cold would get your heart.
He's a hard man. Had us all in the hedges out of sight. There'll
be rheumatism in the Force something horrible on account
of you so we're not in the mood, Adam.

HEPPLE. MacLeish should be here.

GEORGE. See that car on the hill half a mile away? That's him.
He's watching you through binoculars. What did you expect?
Him to dirty his shoes for you, copper-killer? All right, lads,
pack 'em up.

They all go off, ROT, BUNG *shepherded by* GEORGE, *who drags off the cut-outs.*

COWHAND *back on.*

COWHAND. They gone off, and I got them a bite to eat and all.

GEORGE *comes back on.*

GEORGE. What you doing?

COWHAND. Lordy, a bogeyman.

GEORGE. What you hanging round here for? We've had murderers here.

COWHAND. Murderers? God bless me, and I got them a bite to eat.

GEORGE. Did you, now. That could be an offence. Harbouring and abetting criminals, perverting the course of. Could get you for conspiracy, at a pinch.

COWHAND. Oh, dear. I better be off.

GEORGE. You better. Get off out, back to your hayrick. Have no more truck with murderers.

COWHAND. I won't. Lordy, murderers. We're not used to Lond ways round here.

The COWHAND *goes off.*

GEORGE (*aside*). A real bumpkin. But I envy his simple life. Sowing and reaping, seed time and harvest. Dung under your nails and only grass on your mind. Huh. I was raised far away from mother nature. The only farm for miles was for sewage. Fields of tarmac, weeds and tares were all that grew. Human weeds and tares.

Looks around, sniffs, sighs.

The simple life.

Feels his back for rheumatism and turns away, as the lights go down.

Scene Five

The Years Go By.

Lights up, HEPPLE *in his cell. One by one all but* ALBERT
*come forward, speak and do the blood effect, till they are
grouped like a family photograph.*

JANE *comes on.*

JANE. Dad went in again. Brixton. 30 years at Her Majesty's
   pleasure, and she were far from pleased. It all went wrong
   you see, Dad and us. Life too, that went wrong. I got a
   disease. I never went to see about it, I never did. And I died.
   Not at first. Later.

   JANE *puts a blood sack in her mouth, and bleeds.*

   ROT *comes on with* BUNG, *who carries a balloon.*

ROT. Thirty years for each of us. Bung went mad.

   BUNG *comes forward, down on his knees.*

BUNG. Pretty balloon.

   BUNG *bursts the balloon.*

ROT. Went right round the bend in the machine shop. Burst a
   warder's head with his own two hands. Then swallowed a
   pound of three-inch nails.

   BUNG *puts a blood sack in his mouth, and bleeds.*

ROT. As for me, I couldn't stand prison. Got a skin disorder
   like barbed wire. I got a very sensitive

   Pause.

   skin. So I slit my throat with one of the needles they use.
   You know, for mailbags.

   ROT *puts a blood sack in his mouth, and bleeds.*

   LIZ *comes on.*

LIZ. I married old George. Led him a hell of a life. Took in sailors
   when he was on nights.

   Fiercely.

   We needed the extra, he ate so much.

   Change.

One night this sailor went a bit funny and strangled me.

LIZ *puts a blood sack in her mouth, and bleeds.*

GEORGE *comes on.*

GEORGE. A terrible carnage all round. And all within a few years of Adam going down. Like anyone who had to do with him was, how shall I put it? Doomed. I was alright though. I took it very hard about my Lizzie. But I went on for a numbe of years.

Pause.

Then one day I was on traffic duty, when a bus ran over me.

GEORGE *puts a blood sack in his mouth, and bleeds.*

A pause, and they're all in the group.

Then they file off, leaving HEPPLE *alone.*

Scene Six

Hepple's Cell.

HEPPLE. All dead! The Chaplain called in every year or so, telling of the latest to go. Daughters, Rot, Bung, George. I've outlasted all. And me with a heart like a ten-bob watch from Hong Kong. Ha! Life and death, tell me another one.

A clanking of chains, the GHOST OF PC ALBERT *comes on.*

Pause.

HEPPLE. Who are you?

GHOST. I am young Albert's Shade.

HEPPLE. Who?

GHOST. The ghost of the copper you killed.

HEPPLE (*clutches heart briefly, then*): What you want?

GHOST. I was young, my handcuffs were newly oiled, my whistle was bright. You were old. But I died and you lived on. Why?

HEPPLE. Jealous, lad? You should not be. I got a fate far worse. Premature burial. Old folks' home or Brixton Gaol, it's premature burial. The country's full of old 'uns like me, stuffed away.

GHOST. Oh, woe woe, woe woe woe. Your predicament cannot pass ours for agony. We're all down in hell, saying woe woe, woe woe woe. All cos of you. It's not fair, why aren't you dead too? It's offensive to nature. Why haven't you fallen apart, why haven't your bad deeds rotted you away, what keeps you stuck together?

HEPPLE. I'll tell you, spook. Hate. Pure, unadulterated hate keeps me stuck together. Hate. That's my tip for longevity.

GHOST. MacLeish!

HEPPLE. MacLeish!

GHOST. MacLeish!

HEPPLE. I'll get you MacLeish. I'll get him, won't I, spook?

GHOST. Woe.

HEPPLE. Tell me I'll get Revenge.

GHOST. Revenge!

HEPPLE. Revenge!

GHOST. Revenge!

HEPPLE. Revenge! Ah!

A seizure.

GHOST. Woe woe, woe woe woe.

Pause.

HEPPLE. I have abandoned the criminal's dream. What could money get me now? House on the Costa Brava, an easy fuck? What's a house, what's a fuck to an old man? A bit of death, another nail. All those dreams whittled away. Only the one passion left. To stuff MacLeish's truncheon right up his flaming kilt.

GHOST. Adam, look at your cell door.

HEPPLE. It's opened.

GHOST. The guards are asleep. The main gate's ajar.

HEPPLE. What's the game?

GHOST. Go get MacLeish, spend that horrible passion. Then

fall apart for good. Crumble into dirt like you should have long ago, you dirty old bugger . . .

GHOST *goes off with clanking chains.*

Lights go down to blackout.

HEPPLE *actor lights his face with a hand torch, and moves round the stage.*

HEPPLE. All silent. Doors, pushed aside like water. Corridors lit. Not a soul about. By the main gate, two screws asleep. Walked out, like Brixton were mist in the air. Walked through London. All silent. Lit. Not a soul about. Bitter, though.

Hugs himself against the cold.

That's the fence. Them are the bushes. There's the house.

Pause.

Downstairs light off.

He switches his hand torch off.

Must be his Mrs gone up to him.

Lights up.

Scene Seven

MacLeish's Bedroom.

A big wing-backed chair covered in tartan, its back to the audienc[e]. The actor at once does the second quick change, from HEPPLE to MACLEISH.

NOTE. *I'd originally not asked the actor to appear as MACLEISH from the chair until the speech 'Weak now, ineffectual'. Also, to effect the third quick change from MACLEISH back to HEPPLE, I'd put all of MACLEISH's speech from 'I am an old man and bitter' to be done out of sight, but in the first productio[n] John Normington's skill was so considerable MACLEISH was seen almost at once after the second change. He did the third change going out of sight only on 'they're withered away'. H.B.*

The actress playing LIZ doubles as MACLEISH's wife DOROTHY.

DOROTHY. Archie, had your milk?

MACLEISH. What you say, woman?

DOROTHY. Your milk, Archibald.

MACLEISH. Ye stupid old woman, ye old faggot.

DOROTHY. Yes, Archie, have you had your milk?

MACLEISH. I have had my milk.

DOROTHY. And your fingers of bread?

MACLEISH. And my fingers of bread, ye old crone. Ye old withered bagpipes.

DOROTHY. And have you had your pills?

MACLEISH. Yes yes yes yes, ye moulding haggis, ye Aberdeen Angus cow.

DOROTHY. Don't get excited, dearest.

MACLEISH. It's retirement, Dorothy. It unhinges me. Where's my copy of the *Police Gazette.* You've hidden it. You've hidden it away, have you not? Again.

DOROTHY. It works you up so, Archibald.

MACLEISH. Bah, what do you think I am? The child we never had? He had two, you know. Strange the devil's kind should be fertile and God's Elect impotent.

DOROTHY. You weren't impotent, as far as I recollect, religion made you abstemious, but you could do it.

MACLEISH. I could do it! In my day. I am in need of spiritual refreshment. Read me the life of Al Capone.

DOROTHY. You know what the doctor said about that.

MACLEISH. Am I not the master?!

DOROTHY. Yes, dearest. Have a little rest. It's Sunday tomorrow. Listening to the morning service is always a strain.

MACLEISH. Sassenach hereticals!

DOROTHY. Have a little rest.

She goes, switching out the light.

Lights dim a little.

MACLEISH. Weak now. Ineffectual. Lord, desert not your servant in the last of his days. Bah.

Gets out of the chair, fishes under it for whisky bottle and glass. Seizure, then pours a drink shakily and is about to down it when the GHOST OF ALBERT *comes on, with clanking.*

GHOST. Assistant Commissioner, Sir, I am Albert's Ghost. The unhappy Shade of the copper Adam Hepple shot. My murderer stands now in your shrubbery, even where he sent me to my woe. Archibald MacLeish, rise up, deliver your final blow. Rid the earth of that old sinner. I go back on my eternal beat.

GHOST *goes off, with clanking.*

Pause.

MACLEISH. I am an old man and bitter. The only Christian in the Force, and he retired. I fought the good fight. Aye, and lost. Lost, Adam.

Pause.

It's the 1980's now. Rapes every night. No citizen abroad after dark. The coppers armed. Gangs roaming at will, burning down police stations. The country's gone to the devil. You lived before your time, Adam.

Pause.

I had a vision. Jerusalem! Beulah! Judgement! Bah.

Pause.

What you doing here, man? Come for vengeance? What greater vengeance could there be on a man of God, than for God to lose? Eh, Adam?

Pause.

But there're the old scores, are there not?

Pause.

Name them.

Pause.

You cannot. They're withered away. Two old withered cronies we are. Scare you, crow! Scare you, crow!

Senile giggle, pause . . .

Burn, ye Reprobate! Ye'll burn!

At once the actor steps from the chair into a pool of light as HEPPLE. *He carries an axe.*

HEPPLE (*aside*). Bust his shed. Got axe out. Leapt up the
   hanging ivy, like I was young again. In through his bedroom
   window. Tootsied around. Shh. Shh.

Facing the chair, speaking to its hidden side.

Hello, Archie.

Pauses.

You look terrible. Really terrible. Does me good to see how
terrible you look.

Loses control.

You SCABBY JOCK.

Recovers. Turns away.

Pause.

Old scores, Archie. Old bones of contention.

Pause.

Then turns as if MACLEISH *has said 'name them'.*

THE WHOLE RAG BAG.

Pause.

Funny.

Pause.

All these years, dreaming of injuring you. Now you're here
before me, you're just another wormed up old git. That's us,
eh, Archie? Wormed. You by religion, me by prison. What we
doing still alive, being so wormy. Eh?

Pause.

Funny. My dream of a criminal England, it's all come true with
the 1980's. The casino towns, the brothel villages, the cities
red with blood and pleasure. Public life the turn of a card
the fall of a dice. The whole country on the fiddle, the
gamble, the open snatch, the bit on the side. From Land's
End to John O'Groats the whole of England's one giant
pinball table. The ball running wild, Glasgow, Birmingham,
Leeds, Coventry, London, Brighton, Wonderful.

Pause.

We need not have bothered. Ours weren't such a cosmic
struggle, were it, after all. Remember that field where you

nicked me through binoculars. May as well have stayed there. Stuck ourselves up. Like scarecrows.

Senile giggle, pause, suddenly raises the axe.

You COPPER.

Axe on its way down when blackout. At once in the blackout, the two voices from the actor.

HEPPLE. Woke up. Smell of piss. Still in Brixton. Only nightmare died the next day, went down to hell.

MACLEISH. Woke up. Only nightmare. Died next day, ascended into heaven.

	ANATOL
	(translated by Frank Marcus)
Synge	THE PLAYBOY OF THE WESTERN WORLD
	(introduced by T.R. Henn)
Tolstoy	THE FRUITS OF ENLIGHTENMENT
	(translated and introduced by Michael Frayn)
Wedekind	SPRING AWAKENING
	(translated by Edward Bond; introduced by Edward and Elisabeth Bond)
Wilde	THE IMPORTANCE OF BEING EARNEST
	(introduced by Adeline Hartcup)
	LADY WINDERMERE'S FAN
	(introduced by Hesketh Pearson)
Anon	LADY PRECIOUS STREAM
	(adapted by S.I. Hsiung from a sequence of traditional Chinese plays)

If you would like to receive, free of charge, regular information about new plays and theatre books from Methuen, please send your name and address to:

The Marketing Department (Drama)
Methuen London Ltd
North Way
Andover
Hampshire SP10 5BE